MAR 2010

Cows on a Farm

Abbie Mercer

PowerKiDS press

For Hanna Flynn

Published in 2010 by The Rosen Publishing Group, Inc.
29 East 21st Street, New York, NY 10010

Copyright © 2010 by The Rosen Publishing Group, Inc.

All rights reserved. No part of this book may be reproduced in any form without permission in writing from the publisher, except by a reviewer.

First Edition

Editor: Amelie von Zumbusch
Book Design: Kate Laczynski
Photo Researcher: Jessica Gerweck

Photo Credits: Cover, pp. 1, 5, 7, 9, 11, 13, 15, 17, 19, 21, 24 Shutterstock.com; p. 23 flashfilm/Getty Images.

Library of Congress Cataloging-in-Publication Data

Mercer, Abbie.
  Cows on a farm / Abbie Mercer.
    p. cm. — (Barnyard animals)
  Includes index.
  ISBN 978-1-4042-8047-2 (library binding) — ISBN 978-1-4042-8055-7 (pbk.)
ISBN 978-1-4042-8059-5 (6-pack)
  1. Cows—Juvenile literature. I. Title.
  SF208.M47 2010
  636.2—dc22
                                              2008047355

Manufactured in the United States of America

Contents

Meet the Cow 4
A Cow's Life 14
Cows and Milk 20
Words to Know 24
Index 24
Web Sites 24

These large animals are cows. Cows are big and strong, but they are also peaceful.

Cows live on farms like this one. Sometimes, cows stay in outdoor **pastures**.

Cows also stay inside big barns. Barns keep cows safe from bad weather.

Cows come in many colors, such as white, brown, and black.

Many cows, such as this baby cow, have color **patterns** on their coats.

13

Baby cows are called **calves**. Mother cows most often have one calf at a time.

15

A group of cows is called a herd. Cows get along well with the other members of their herds.

Cows eat mostly **hay**. When they are outside, cows also eat grass.

People drink milk from cows. Milk is good for you.

People also make cheese and ice cream from milk. Cows are helpful animals!

Words to Know

calf

hay

pasture

pattern

Index

M
members, 16
milk, 20, 22

P
pastures, 6

patterns, 12
people, 20, 22

W
weather, 8

Web Sites

Due to the changing nature of Internet links, PowerKids Press has developed an online list of Web sites related to the subject of this book. This site is updated regularly. Please use this link to access the list:
www.powerkidslinks.com/byard/cows/

24